AF797403

Alternative Employee Ownership Structures

Christopher T. Horner II, Cynthia A. Moore, and Corey Rosen

The National Center for Employee Ownership (NCEO)

Visit **www.nceo.org** for more information about employee ownership, ownership culture, and leadership

Alternative Employee Ownership Structures

Christopher T. Horner II, Cynthia A. Moore, and Corey Rosen

Book design by Scott Rodrick

The National Center for Employee Ownership
(510) 208-1300
www.nceo.org

978-1-954990-16-6

Contents

Introduction

Corey Rosen

EMPLOYEE OWNERSHIP is very common in the U.S. According to the General Social Survey, about one-third of the employees who work for companies with stock own stock in their company in one way or another. Much has been written about the most common forms of sharing ownership widely with employees (ESOPs, stock and stock rights grants, qualified stock purchase plans, and 401(k) plans with company stock as an investment or matching option). But there are other ways that companies can share ownership widely with employees that get less media and professional attention. This book looks at a number of alternative structures, including nonqualified broad-based stock purchase plans, profit sharing plans invested substantially in employer stock, internal stock markets, and what we call "legacy plans"—plans that have unique structures set up specifically for that company. We also discuss worker cooperatives. Although these have been written about widely, they are far less common than the other main forms of employee ownership, but do represent an alternative worth considering that is not much discussed in the business press.

Conventional Forms of Ownership Sharing

The very large majority of employees who own stock in their companies do so in four ways:

ESOPs. ESOPs are tax-qualified retirement plans specifically designed for broad-based employee ownership. ESOPs have been given substantial tax benefits by Congress. They are by far the most tax-efficient way both to share ownership and to provide for business continuity in closely held companies. There are over 13 million participants in ESOPs. In return for the tax benefits granted to companies and employees, ESOPs must adhere to strict rules concerning eligibility, allocation, vesting, valuation, and distribution. ESOPs hold shares for employees in a trust. ESOPs almost always acquire shares from tax-deductible contributions from the employer. ESOPs are also the only employee ownership plan that can borrow money from the company or on its credit to buy shares.

Individual equity awards. About 9 million employees hold stock options, stock appreciation rights, restricted stock, or phantom stock. These awards provide either the right to acquire shares or actual shares, almost always subject to some vesting rule. There are few requirements as to how companies decide who is eligible, what they will get, and on what terms they will get the awards. These plans generally do not carry any special tax advantages for companies. With incentive stock options, employees who hold the shares for at least one year after exercise and two years after grant receive long-term capital gains tax treatment on the increase in value between the price they pay and the price at which they sell the stock.

Qualified employee stock purchase plans. These plans allow employees to buy shares at a discount of up to 15%. Employees put after-tax money aside out of payroll over an offering period that can last from 3 months to 27 months, at the option of the employer. Companies can allow employees to take the discount based on just the price at the end of the offering period or the lower of the prices at the beginning and end. Employees can get beneficial tax treatment if they hold the shares for both one year after the purchase and two years after the beginning of the offering period. Plans must be broadly available to all employees with two years or more of service, with certain exceptions.

401(k) plans. About one-third of public companies offer employer stock in their 401(k) plans, usually as an investment option but sometimes as a match or both. About 7.5% of all 401(k) assets are in employer stock.

Alternative Plans Discussed Here

The above plans are not the only way employees can become owners, however. This book looks at a variety of other options:

Nonqualified stock purchase plans. In these plans, companies allow employees to purchase shares with after-tax dollars. Companies can provide the right to any employee on virtually any terms. Current securities law allow all but the largest privately held companies to offer broad-based purchase plans without having to comply with complex and expensive securities laws.In the examples profiled here, companies use a variety of approaches to nonqualified stock purchase plans. Eligibility, terms of purchase, pricing, resale options, and other features are all up to the company. This flexibility is appealing, but these plans carry no special tax benefits. While nonqualified purchase plans can be found in all kinds of companies, their use for broad-based ownership (ownership by more than just managers and other key employees) is most common in engineering and architecture firms, as well as some other firms where the companies' primary assets are the special skills of individual employees.

Internal stock markets. These markets are simply a more sophisticated take on nonqualified stock purchase plans. While those plans provide liquidity by allowing other employees to buy shares and/or the company buying shares, they do not offer a formal market for these transactions where employees can buy and sell shares at set intervals at determined prices with the company acting as a buyer or seller of shares to clear the market. These kinds of plans can be costly to operate for very large companies, but one example here, TEOCO, found a way to make them work efficiently on a smaller scale.

Legacy plans. There are a handful of "one-off" employee ownership plans that usually reflect some long-term legacy by founding owners committed to employee ownership. These plans are idiosyncratic. They may limit the value of shares and focus on dividends instead; they may hold the shares in a permanent trust for the benefit of employees. There are very few of these plans, but they provide alternative models that may work well for some situations.

Worker cooperatives. Worker cooperatives are the most democratic form of employee ownership. They require that only employees be owners of voting shares (or membership interests) and that everyone have just one vote. They do not have any special tax benefits. Some worker cooperatives have shares or membership interests that are at fixed values that do not fluctuate with the value of the company; others allow prices to rise and fall. Almost all have some form of internal accounts that provide at least some of the annual profit in the form of a distribution to employees in cash and to an account held in their name to be paid out at a later point. There are thousands of worker cooperatives in the U.S., but they typically are very small.

Profit sharing plans and stock bonus plans. The most common option to ESOPs is a profit sharing plan. There are about 4,000 profit sharing plans with 30% or more of their assets in employer stock, although only about 700 of these have 10 or more employees. As explained later in this book, these very small plans are probably not designed for broad-based employee ownership, but we believe most of the larger ones are. While most of even the 700 companies are still relatively small, there are some larger employers, including some profiled here.

Profit sharing plans are, like ESOPs, qualified retirement plans, meaning they have to meet rules for eligibility, allocation, vesting, and distribution designed to assure equitable treatment of employees. They do not have any of the special tax benefits granted to ESOPs but they also have less strict requirements concerning valuation, distribution, asset holdings, and other issues. For companies not needing the special tax benefits, profit sharing plans may be more appealing.

Stock bonus plans were once popular as employee ownership vehicles, but have become uncommon today. Their rules are very similar to ESOPs, but, over time, ESOPs tax benefits have become increasingly attractive compared to those available to stock bonus plans.

The remainder of this book looks at these various plans in more detail. For each kind of plan, there is a chapter describing how the plans work followed by brief case studies exemplifying the various approaches. Because profit sharing plans are such a common alternative to ESOPs for broad-based employee ownership, we have included a detailed legal look at how these plans compare to ESOPs in the final chapter of this book.

1

Nonqualified Stock Purchase Plans

Corey Rosen

QUALIFIED EMPLOYEE STOCK PURCHASE PLANS are those that meet the rules under Section 423 of the Internal Revenue Code. They allow participating employees to get capital gains tax treatment on the sale of their shares if certain rules are met. Qualified stock purchase plans must be available to all employees (except 5% owners, who are ineligible) except highly compensated employees, those working 20 hours or less per week, and those with less than two years of service. The right to purchase stock under the plan must accrue at a rate of no more than $25,000 per year. Many companies want employees to be owners through a stock purchase arrangement but want more flexibility than qualified plans provide. Because companies can structure stock purchase plans in almost any way they choose, there are a variety of models for this. The profiles below discuss how seven different companies with very different workforces structured their plans.

Securities law changes have made it easier to offer these plans without incurring expensive and burdensome registration requirements. The complex details of these laws, however, are beyond the scope of this discussion.

Journal Communications

Journal Communications is a publicly traded, Milwaukee-based publisher of the *Milwaukee Journal-Sentinel* as well as the owner of several media outlets. The company went public in 2003, but employees remain its largest owners.

The company's employee ownership plans date back to 1937. Publisher Harry Grant believed that "it is the right of men and women whose lives go into building a newspaper to have a share in its ownership." Grant and Faye MacBeath, another owner of the company, made 30,000 stock "units" available to employees, amounting to a 25% interest. That grew gradually to 55% by in 1947, 80% by 1964, and 90% in the 1980s. A voting trust held the remaining shares.

Unlike stock, units could be sold only to other employees. Voting rights on the units were limited. These rules changed after the company went public, as explained below.

Employees can buy units after three years of service. Each year, employees are able to buy a certain number of units. The president of the company decides on how much people can get, with allotment recommendations from department heads. Guidelines include length of service, salary, and responsibility level. The goal is for all employees to be able to buy units.

The units (now called class B shares) are valued based on a formula that starts with the book value of common stock, adds net income for the year, subtracts dividends paid, then multiplies that by a number that reflects a multiple of net income available for dividends over the prior five years. Employees can buy the units out of cash or money in the company's profit sharing plan. Employees can also borrow money from the company's credit unions for up to 80% of the value of the purchase.

Until the company went public, employees could sell to other employees at any time at the unit option price. When an employee retired, the units could be sold in installments over time. Dividends were (and still are) paid on units in the same way they are to other shareholders. About a third of the employees buy shares, and many of them have ended up doing very well.

The cash employees gave to the company was an important source of working capital. Most of that was borrowed. In 2003, the outstanding loans came to $430 million. The company was under pressure to increase dividends to allow employees to pay for the loans. The solution to this dilemma, the company's directors decided, was to go public. Publicly owned shares have very limited voting rights.

Since the public offering, the percentage of equity held by employees has shrunk to about 8.5% of total shares. The units (now Class B shares), however, have 10 votes per share. Employees are now to convert their shares to class A shares at their option, but only after first offering to sell them to other eligible purchasers.

Kimley-Horn

Raleigh, North Carolina-based Kimley-Horn is an engineering design consulting firm, ranked number 39 on the *Engineering News-Record*'s list of the top 500 design consulting firms. The founders of the company, which was started in 1967, believed it was a good idea to allow key employees to have the opportunity for ownership. Their core concept was that it was better to own a small piece of a large company than a large piece of small one. The approach has served the company well: today it has over 1,800 employees (with roughly 20% being shareholders) and a well-functioning employee ownership transition plan. By design, the firm's shares are broadly distributed among its shareholders. No one person owns more than 7% of the outstanding stock.

At Kimley-Horn, ownership transition is an ongoing process, not a periodic event. Twice a year the firm completes a formal process to identify employees for ownership and other promotion steps. The process begins at the grassroots level as local and regional leaders recommend employees who are reviewed by firm leaders and ultimately approved by the firm's board of directors. In addition, existing shareholders are given the opportunity to purchase additional shares of stock annually, with the number of shares offered being determined by the board of directors. In this way, shareholders are able to grow their investment in the firm over time.

Based on their contributions to the firm's success, employees are able to move along a "Path to Ownership" that includes being named an associate and being offered the opportunity to purchase debentures before being named a shareholder. Debentures are interest-bearing notes between the employee and the firm that allow employees to save money for the purchase of shares when they are offered. Employees generally fund their purchases of debentures and shares of stock from their incentive bonuses.

All shareholders sign a master contract that sets the formula upon which the share price is determined as well as other key provisions such as the requirement to sell their shares back to the firm upon the end of employment or age 67.

Ownership transition is often a challenging topic for professional services firms. Kimley-Horn provides an example of how a well-functioning employee ownership plan can allow a firm to move seamlessly from one generation to another, enhance staff retention, and entice potential employees.

Robert W. Baird

Robert W. Baird & Co. is a Milwaukee, Wisconsin-based financial services company. Ranked number 9 on the 2014 *Fortune* 100 Best Companies to Work For list, 80% of its stock is owned by non-senior management employees and 14% by senior managers. It employs close to 3,000 people worldwide, primarily in the U.S. Approximately 55% of the employees own stock.

Founded in 1919, Baird was an independent company until 1982, when it became a part of the Northwestern Mutual family of companies. In 1998, Baird began a program to increase employee ownership, reaching 36% by the end of that year and 45% in 2001. In 2004, it bought out the remaining Northwestern Mutual shares, leaving almost all the ownership in the hands of employees. Baird has a very employee-centered culture, with over 200 applications per job opening. The firm's voluntary turnover is 5.5%, compared to an industry average of 12%.

Marianne Foster, a public relations specialist at Baird, told the NCEO that as an associate-owned firm:

> All Baird associates have the opportunity to buy stock if they meet the eligibility criteria:
>
> - Associates must have three years of Baird service as of December 31 in the year in which they are nominated or hold an officer title of vice president or higher. Some Baird business units have additional requirements.
> - Associates must be regular full-time or part-time associates.
> - Associates must have made significant contributions to Baird's current success and be willing to be an active participant in the firm's anticipated growth.

Committees in each of Baird's business units and in its Corporate Resource Group vote on the new shareholder nominees at the end of each year. Existing shareholders and associates invited to become shareholders are offered the opportunity to purchase common shares through the annual remarketing process. Shares are bought and sold at a price that reflects fair market value as determined by Baird management. The minimum stock purchase is 50 shares. The availability of shares is at the discretion of senior management and is driven by a number of considerations.

SpawGlass Holdings

In the early 1990s when a French multinational wanted to sell its U.S. holdings, Ron Taylor, an officer with the U.S. operations, proposed it sell the businesses to employees. At first, the company said the employees couldn't afford them, so Taylor talked the company into trying it just with one of the businesses the multinational wanted to sell, the company now known as SpawGlass Employee Holdings.

In many cases, the sale of the Texas construction company might have been structured as an ESOP, but in this case, the French owners wanted to limit their liability going forward through a simple deal that could get them out of the business quickly. In May 1993, a deal was finalized in which 51% of the Texas-based company was sold to 10 managers. The multinational retained the rest of the company. Over time the number of owners grew. The company, which remains private, is now 100% employee-owned and has 300 shareholders, 60% of its work force. SpawGlass employs over 500 people. It provides construction management design-build, and civil contractor services. The firm is annually ranked among Texas' top workplaces. Its client base includes healthcare, oil and gas, public works, commercial, senior living, student housing, higher education, civil construction as well as other facility types.

The road from management ownership to broad-based ownership happened in stages. Taylor, who became chairman and CEO of SpawGlass, told the NCEO that the managers who owned the stock decided to cultivate an ownership culture first. So they went to NCEO and Great Game of Business seminars. They started using open-book management and educating employees about how the business worked. And they added shares to their existing bonus plan. That first year, salaried employees received 20 shares as part of their annual bonuses and gained the right to buy shares in the company through payroll deductions. The employees had the right to sell the bonus related shares back to the company immediately, but most didn't. That year, the number of shareholders jumped to the high 30s.

Company executives started asking themselves why the hourly employees weren't being included. The company is a non-union open shop, so it did not have to negotiate the issue. Although some were concerned that turnover was too high among the hourly employees for stock ownership to be practical, an analysis showed that if hourly employees made it past an initial period, they tended to stay just as long as salaried employees. So the company started offering bonuses and the right to purchase stock to hourly employees, using the same system as for salaried ones.

Under the resulting plan, all employees can have as much after-tax pay as they choose withheld from their paychecks to buy additional stock. Eligibility begins at the first stock-buying opportunity after someone joins the company, usually the first day of the quarter. The company has worked with a bank to help employees finance stock purchases through loans if they so choose. Employees must sell the stock back to the company when they leave, but in the meantime they reap dividends.

Chain Store

This company (which is unnamed here because it requested anonymity) is group of over 50 stores, with 10 to 12 planned to be added per year for the next several years. The company's ownership structure is unusual. It was started by partners opening two stores, then bringing on people who opened additional stores. New stores might be owned by the people who had already started some of the existing stores and/or by new partners. An umbrella company acted as the employer for all the stores and provided administrative, marketing, and purchasing support. Eventually, an e-commerce division was added.

In the early 2000s they opened a new store and let employees buy in to the umbrella corporation. Nonvoting shares were bought and sold at book value. Later, this program was extended to a handful of additional existing stores for selected store management employees. More recently, the program was extended to more stores and opened up to any employee working 20 hours of more per week. There are fairly substantial limits set for how much hourly, salaried, and managerial employees can buy. Employees can sell their shares at book value when they leave the company. The return on shares has been impressive, more than twice the S&P 500 for the last several years.

The goal now is to continue to extend the program to more employees and stores and to bring individual store ownership under the corporate umbrella. The company has looked at an ESOP, but decided, for now, not to pursue it. Management was concerned about how the appraised price would be very different from the book value price, how ESOP rules would give them less discretion over eligibility and ownership amounts, and costs they were told would be a few hundred thousand dollars per year.

These costs, of course, are well above what actual annual costs would be (probably under $50,000 per year). It is also possible for an ESOP to be designed so that all employees are eligible to buy shares, and that this is the only way the ESOP is funded. As long as the offer is nondiscriminatory, employees can put in varying amounts.

The Sky Factory

The Sky Factory is a 35-employee company in Fairfield, Iowa, that creates "illusions of nature," such as sky ceilings, luminous windows, and other artifices that create a sense of the outdoors indoors. Bill Witherspoon, the company's founder, says employee ownership has been the key to the company's success.

The company is made up mostly of artists as well as some engineers. Witherspoon believes that these people need entrepreneurial freedom and a sense of co-ownership in order to stay with the company. The company is deeply committed to open-book management and employee involvements. Witherspoon told *Inc.* Magazine in 2010 that "as a company of owners, everyone who works here is naturally motivated to participate in important decisions. To do so, people have to know everything. . . . On Fridays, we have a two-hour meeting. For the first 30 minutes, we go over all the metrics. In addition to the critical numbers, people will raise questions about how many problems we've had that week or how many architects our marketers visited. We track all of that and maintain a historical record of the data that anyone can see at any time. Everyone is trained in financial literacy so he or she can make the best use of the information." All significant decisions are made by consensus.

Employees can buy shares annually. The amount they can buy is based on how much the company grows that year. Shares are bought with after-tax dollars or a promissory note and held individually. The share price is based on an annual valuation. The stock is discounted by 80%, which means employees would have a tax liability on the discounted amount. Employees are able to buy stock annually, with the percentage of stock available based on the company's growth for that year. The company buys back the shares at the appraised price when employees leave.

In addition to ownership, each month the company distributes 50% of the net profit to everyone, provided there have been no late shipments since the last bonus, cash does not drop below six months' operating expenses, and there has been positive cash flow for the previous 12 weeks. The formula is salary divided by total salaries.

Chroma Technology

Chroma Technology is a Brattleboro, Vermont, manufacturer of "interference filters for the ultra-violet, visible and near-infrared portions of the spectrum." These optical filters are used in applications such as biomedical imaging, DNA sequencing, and fluorescent microscopy by hospitals, universities, and research facilities.

In 1991 Chroma Technology was formed by a group of six people. The founders wanted to work for themselves, so they modeled their ownership like a law firm. Initially, the salaries were all set at $30,000. Each founder purchased and received 1,000 shares of stock.

As the company grew and added new people, they used the same approach. New employees were partners as well, with the same salary and benefits. Each year, Chroma pays workers a bonus that is to be used to purchase 200 shares in the company. Voting power is keyed to share size, so workers with the most seniority have the greatest say.

Strategic decisions are made by the company's board, which consists of the six founders as well as three members elected by all the workers.

Employees are able to cash out up to 25% of their shares with no penalty while they are still working. Vice President Paul Millman says that the firm rejected the ESOP approach because "it's essentially a retirement plan and expensive to manage."

Profits continue to be split equally amongst the owners based on salary. Gradually, Chroma moved away from a completely flat salary structure to four tiers, but compensation differences are still relatively compressed.

2

Internal Markets

Corey Rosen

SETTING UP an internal stock market for employees to buy and sell shares has traditionally been a very difficult and expensive process. Generally, a company must register as a broker-dealer (that is, acting as an agent for the buying and selling of shares) both with the Securities and Exchange Commission and each state in which it operates. Although most states use a uniform code for securities regulations, the compliance costs, both financial and in terms of time, are substantial. Companies may also need to register their securities with the SEC, requiring significant and regular disclosure requirements similar to those for publicly traded companies.

There are two practical exceptions that a company can use. The recent Jumpstart Our Business (JOBS) Act (passed in 2012) may make it easier to simplify these requirements. Prior law allowed unregistered public offerings of up to $5 million of securities in a 12-month period, including no more than $1.5 million of securities offered by security holders of the company, including current employees. That would limit the usefulness of the exemption in all but fairly small companies. Prior rules also required compliance with state blue sky laws, including reporting and broker-dealer rules.

Regulation A requires companies to submit an offering statement that is then reviewed by the SEC staff. The rules for this are made simpler for qualifying companies, however. Current Regulation A offerings also are subject to state-level registration and qualification requirements. The JOBS Act requires the SEC to develop rules for an expanded exemption allowing offerings of up to $50 million of securities within a 12-month period; as of this writing, those rules had not been finalized. Companies would be required to file audited financial statements with the SEC, but other reporting requirements would be simpler. Companies may also be exempt, at least to some degree, from blue sky laws, but, as of this writing, this is still uncertain.

Companies that choose not to use the Regulation A exemption may be able to use an exemption under Rule 701 of the Securities Act of 1933, as in the case of TEOCO presented below. Under federal law, offers to a company's employees, directors, general partners, trustees, officers, or certain consultants (those providing services to a company similar to what an employer might hire someone to do, but not consultants who help raise capital) can be made under a written compensation agreement. If total sales during a 12-month period do not exceed the greater of (1) $1 million, (2) 15% of the issuer's total assets, or (3) 15% of all the outstanding securities of that class, then the offerings are exempt from registration requirements. The offerings must be discrete (not included in any other offer) and are still subject to disclosure requirements. For total sales not exceeding $5 million during a 12-month period to the specified class of people above, companies must comply with anti-fraud disclosure rules; for sales over this amount, companies must disclose additional information, including risk factors, copies of the plans under which the offerings are made, and certain financial statements. These disclosures must be made to all shareholders.

For purposes of this rule, options are considered part of the aggregate sales price, with the option price defined as of the date of grant. In calculating outstanding securities for the 15% rule, all currently exercisable or convertible options, warrants, rights, and other securities are counted.

We know of very few companies that have set up internal markets. The two cases below illustrate both the conventional approach and a much simpler approach that allowed a company to avoid the broker-dealer requirements.

TEOCO: Simplifying the Internal Market

TEOCO (The Employee Owned Company) is a "provider of assurance and analytics solutions to communications service providers worldwide." The company was founded in 1994 out of the commitment of the founder, Atul Jain, to create a company with the highest commitment to business ethics. Part of that commitment was to create a model of shared success. That extends to profit sharing, a stock purchase plan, an ESOP, and shared decision making. Jain believes the environment created by employee ownership leads to better performance and stronger employee commitment.

The results seem to bear him out. TEOCO has grown to over 1,400 employees with offices in 15 countries. Its 2014 revenues are about $180 million, with impressive profitability. It consistently has been included on *Inc.* magazine's list of the fastest-growing private companies and Deloitte's Technology's Fast 500. It grew 197% in 2013. Companies with track records like these in the technology sector often either go public or find a buyer willing to pay a large premium. Either would be an option for TEOCO, but Jain prefers to stay private, in large part to maintain the culture he and his fellow employees have worked so hard to build. In 2011 Jain was named one of the 25 most influential people in the communications software world by *Billing and OSS World*.

Initially, the only ownership vehicle was stock purchases. Jain broke with the traditional technology company model of giving out stock options because he believed stock purchases led to a greater commitment. Over time, that model has changed.

Because of varying laws in the countries where it operates, not all these plans are available in every country, although all employees get stock options.

One element of TEOCO's shared ownership model is the annual bonus, paid to all employees. The bonus is essentially a profit sharing plan in that it is not discretionary as to who gets what amounts. Instead, a bonus pool of 15% of pretax profits is set aside, with a target of 8% of base pay for all employees other than certain key people who get a higher percentage up to 20% to 40%. Employees can choose to receive up to 60% of their bonus in shares. Jain limited the percentage to 60% to make sure people would have money to pay taxes. "Otherwise," he said, "they might get 100% in shares, find they have to pay their taxes, but the share price could go down, leaving them underwater and unhappy."

In addition to bonuses, all employees receive stock options. How much they get depends on their role in the company. There is also an ESOP for U.S. employees. In 2012 it had 251 participants and about $650,000 in assets. The ESOP is used to match employee 401(k) deferrals.

Another opportunity for ownership is an employee stock purchase plan. The purchase of shares can be done with the employee's own funds or out of payroll deductions monthly until end of the year. At the end of six months, deferrals are translated into shares. There is a limit of $500 per month or 10% of salary, whichever is less, on how much can be purchased.

TEOCO's most interesting innovation, however, is its internal market. Early on, every employee could buy up to a specific number of shares, but as the price kept going up, that became more difficult. Instead, TEOCO began to limit the total dollar amount that could be purchased. At first, it was $10,000 per year. Now it is $5,000 and will be reduced further, probably to $2,500. Jain says the limit is to prevent the "rich uncle" syndrome where some people are able to buy a lot more stock than others. Now that TEOCO has multiple ownership mechanisms, the limit is less constraining in terms of how much employees own overall in shares. The shares are bought and sold on an internal market.

Until recently, the process of operating an internal market seemed too daunting for all but the largest employers. The consensus was that companies had to register as broker-dealers wherever they operated. In

2011, TEOCO found a way to make this more practical. In its internal market, TEOCO arranges for periodic trades, currently once a year. A plan committee oversees the process. Dates are set in advance, detailed information mailed to employees, and an informational meeting held. Employees can offer to sell shares they own or buy additional shares. The company establishes minimums and maximums on the number of shares that must be purchased or can be sold. The company acts as the sole buyer and seller, rather than the transactions occurring between individuals. An independent third-party appraiser sets the sale price in advance, but it must be revisited if there are material changes in the interim. Employees indicate how many shares they want to sell or buy and submit this to the company. In the unlikely event the number of sale and purchase offers is equal; the company buys all the shares for sale and resells them all. More likely, there will be an imbalance. If there are more purchase offers, the company buys all the shares for sale, then parcels them out based on an equitable formula designed to give preference to smaller holders. If there are more sellers, the company accepts all offers to buy then allocates the remaining number according to the same formula. Because the company is buying and selling for its own account, not acting as an agent (especially a commissioned agent) of the sellers or buyers, the SEC accepted the argument that it is not a broker-dealer. The company also will not need to register the shares because of an exemption for sales to employees under Rule 701, which exempts from registration offers of 15% or less of a company's equity to employees in a 12-month period.

Combining all these plans, employees own about 16% to 17% of the company. That number has been higher in the past, but a major investment in the company by an outside firm reduced the percentage, but not the value, which has continued to rise rapidly.

CH2M HILL

CH2M HILL is a 26,000-employee consulting, design, design-build, operations, and program management company operating on six continents. Based in Colorado, the company is entirely owned by its employees, primarily through stock purchases through an internal stock market. The company also provides stock options to selected employees and an employee stock purchase plan (ESPP) that allows employees to buy a specified number of shares annually at a 10% discount. Those shares can be sold on the internal market. The regulatory compliance costs of the program are substantial given that the company operates in multiple states and countries. The company believes the costs are well justified by the returns. The material below is based on the company's 2010 Form S-8 registration statement filed with the SEC (which was the company's the most recent S-8 listed on the SEC's EDGAR system as of this writing). CH2M HILL has no publicly traded stock. Employees, directors, and selected consultants can own stock.

Shares are bought and sold through an internal market operated by a registered broker-dealer under applicable federal, state, and international laws. The board of directors "based on our after-tax profits, otherwise referred to as net income, and shareholders' equity, as well as a subjective analysis of market factors." The company can buy and sell shares on periodic trade dates to balance the supply and demand for our common stock between sellers and buyers, but is not obligated to do so. Shareholders can offer to sell or purchase shares on four trade dates each year. The company can set a limit on the number of shares an individual may buy. The company's S-8 filing notes that the decision about whether to clear the market if there is an imbalance of sell and buy offers is "solely within our discretion and we will not notify investors as to whether or not we will participate prior to the Trade Date." Valuation focuses on profit and book value, but is adjusted for market factors, including: "The market for publicly traded equity securities of companies comparable to us . . . The merger and acquisition market for companies comparable to us . . . The prospects for our future performance . . . General economic conditions . . . General capital market conditions . . . [and] Other factors our Board of Directors deem appropriate." The board may also consider an independent appraisal by an outside appraisal firm.

In addition to the internal market, the company offers a tax-qualified employee stock purchase plan (ESPP). Employees put aside money over a year out of payroll deductions and can purchase shares at the end of the one-year offering period at a 10% discount. Selected employees also are eligible for stock options. The internal market has been very successful for the company, with the large majority of employees participating. That is not surprising given that the company has grown from 500 employees in 1969 to 26,000 today. The company is consistently ranked as one of the 100 Best Companies to Work For America, as compiled for *Fortune* by the Great Place to Work Institute.

This chapter is drawn in part from an interview with Atul Jain and in part from information in Thomas J. Calo and Frank Shipper, "Principled Entrepreneurship and Shared Leadership: The Case of TEOCO (The Employee Owned Company)," Journal of Business Case Studies *8, no. 1 (January/February 2012).*

3

Legacy Plans

Corey Rosen

THERE ARE A HANDFUL OF COMPANIES that have plans that go far back, well before ESOPs. They have unique structures based on the values of the people who originally set them up and would not easily fit into an ESOP model.

Graybar

Clayton, Missouri-based Graybar Electric, a Fortune 500 company, is an electrical distributor with 8,400 employees. Like American Cast Iron Pipe Company, its shares are held entirely in a trust. Unlike American Cast Iron Pipe Company, however, the Graybar trust fixes the price at $20 per share in perpetuity. The unusual structure goes back to 1929, when its employees bought it from Western Electric. Western Electric provided generous terms, and most of the 1,700 employees at the time bought shares. The sale was so unusual that it receive substantial national press coverage.

Under the terms of the trust, stock can only be purchased by employees. Employees can sell the stock back to the company at termination or hold onto it after retirement and sell later. The company retains the option to buy the shares and always does. Rather than the share price going up and down, earnings are attributed to the shares each year as a dividend. They accumulate in the trust in the employee's name and, at payout, the employee gets the $20 plus the accumulated dividends. There was a 20% dividend in 2013; over the prior 20 years, dividends amounted to about a 10% annual return.

Offerings are made pursuant to a prospectus filed with the Securities and Exchange Commission. The company makes available a number of shares the board determines is appropriate for that year's needs. All full-time employees and retirees can purchase shares. An installment plan is available. The number of shares available is based on a formula. In 2013 it was one share for each $550 of annual base salary increased by a multiple, as described below in the prospectus:

- Executives EX1 through EX5 3.00
- Grades 17, 18, 19 and 20 and Band M1 2.50
- Grades 15 and 16 and Band M2 2.25
- Grades P and Q 1.90
- Grades N and O 1.85
- Grade 14 or below covered either by the Management Incentive Plan or the Sales Incentive Plan and Band M3 1.75
- Grades J, K, L and M 1.50
- All others 1.25

Under the voting trust agreement, the prospectus says that employees have the right to elect the board and vote on all matters shareholders vote on. However, the terms of the trust also specify that "the Voting Trustees are entitled in their discretion and using their best judgment to vote all the shares deposited in the Voting Trust with respect to the election of directors and the ratification, approval or disapproval of any other action or proposed action of Graybar requiring a vote or consent by shareholders, except that the Voting Trustees may not vote on the merger or consolidation of Graybar into or with another corporation, the sale of all or substantially all of our assets or our liquidation or dissolution without the consent of the holders of Voting Trust Interests representing at least 75% of the aggregate number of shares then deposited." The voting rules, then, look much like those of an ESOP.

American Cast Iron Pipe Company

American Cast Iron Pipe Company was founded by John Joseph Egan in Birmingham, Alabama. As a devout Christian, Eagan had a strong commitment to values of fairness and opportunity. The company was a pioneer in race relations and employee benefits. It was one of the first companies to offer a pension plan, something it still does today. In 1924, Eagan willed ownership of the company in a trust to its employees. Management of the company is performed by a 14-person board of operatives, 12 elected by hourly employees, 1 elected by salaried employees, and 1 elected by all employees. This group serves as an advisory organization to management, and 4 members serve on the company board along with executives and outsiders. They meet with management every other week.

Egan believed that "Industry has no right to use the best years of a man's life and, as old age approaches, throw him out. It is one of the real joys to see men receiving monthly their own money which has been set aside for them." Bequeathing the company to employees was the ultimate way for him to express that sentiment.

The trust holds the beneficial ownership of the shares in perpetuity. Employees do not buy or sell shares from the trust, nor do they hold individual accounts in it. Instead, they receive dividends on the ownership, amounting to about 10% of pay in recent years. All employees are eligible for the plan.

Note: The NCEO contacted the company to ask for more details on eligibility and allocation, but it did not respond. Because this is an interesting model, we included this limited information here.

4

Worker Cooperatives

Corey Rosen

WORKER COOPERATIVES are organizations democratically controlled by their members on a one-person, one-vote basis. Several states have a specific worker cooperative statute, but in most states, worker cooperatives are organized as conventional corporations that limit voting to members on a one-member, one-vote basis. In states with cooperative statutes, there is less uncertainty about taxation and governance issues, but cooperatives in other states have generally been easily able to find appropriate statutes to accommodate their structure. Cooperatives are not subject to any special tax treatment except in the case of a sale of a closely held company to a qualifying worker cooperative (most notably one that owns at least 50% of the company and whose employees control the company on a one-member, one-vote basis). In these cases, sellers can defer taxation on the sale by reinvesting in other securities. This is the same law—Section 1042 of the Internal Revenue Code—that sellers to qualifying ESOPs can use.

In the past, worker cooperatives were like any other shareholder-owned company except that only workers could buy shares and only owners could be workers. Moreover, each employee was limited to owning one share. Employees would buy into the company out of their savings or deductions from payroll over time. The share value fluctuated with the value of the company, so successful worker cooperatives found that new employees were often unable to afford the shares. Many of these companies ended up being sold. The companies could also hire non-owning employees.

Today, worker cooperatives more commonly limit the value of the equity. While technically employees are buying a share of the company, they are actually buying a membership in the cooperative. This can be priced at any dollar value, but it is usually a few thousand dollars and can be financed out of wages over time. Typically, new employees have a probation period before being voted in to be able to buy a membership interest. Each member has one vote. The membership interest is held until the employee leaves, when it is repaid, sometimes with interest.

The share value does not fluctuate over time, other than any added interest. This prevents the cooperative from facing the kind of repurchase crisis that earlier worker cooperatives did but may also mean employees will be more focused on short-term profits than long-term growth. As the excellent resource on worker cooperatives *In Good Company: A Guide to Worker Cooperatives* (North Country Development Fund, 2006) points out, "For a fast growing or highly successful business, this literal allocation of profit dollars does nothing to capture the ongoing value of the business, and therefore tends to severely underestimate the value of a successful business over time. Large, very successful cooperatives have often eventually made the decision to sell to a competitor at market value and cease to be a cooperative because the total dollar value of the stock in members' accounts was so clearly and substantially below the market value of the assets that made up the cooperative and selling the business was the only way to realize the present value of those future earnings."

Cooperatives typically divide their profits between two accounts: a collective account that holds retained earnings for the cooperative as a whole (much like retained earnings in a conventional company) and individual member accounts that have a share of earnings allocated to them (much like a profit sharing trust in a conventional company).

Unlike a profit sharing trust, however, there are no rules on how the profits are divided, but generally in worker cooperatives it would be equally based on hours. Tax law requires that when the portion of the profits is allocated, it is taxable to the employee whether received or not. Cooperatives are thus typically required to distribute at least 20% of the allocation in cash to allow members to pay their taxes. The remainder of the allocated earnings is paid out either periodically or when the employee leaves.

Worker cooperatives are much more commonly used in start-ups than in business transitions. Their low cost of organization, their ability to obtain initial equity from their members, their enhanced commitment to making the business successful that a worker cooperative can provide, and their philosophical appeal both to some potential entrepreneurs and funders can make them an appealing start-up model in the right circumstances.

This discussion on worker cooperatives is necessarily cursory. There are a number of variations on the worker cooperative model, including share price valuation; allowing for equity investors to buy preferred, not voting stock; limitations on non-member workers; governance principles aside from one-member, one-vote; and more. *In Good Company: A Guide to Worker Cooperatives* (mentioned above) is the best resource we have found on these alternative choices.

South Mountain

One of the most successful and enduring worker cooperatives is South Mountain Company in West Tisbury, Massachusetts, an environmentally responsible architecture, building, and renewable energy company founded in 1975. The following is an edited excerpt, by founder John Abrams (who is president and CEO today), from the detailed company history on its Web site that describes the development of its cooperative over time. More detail is provided in John Abrams' book, *Companies We Keep*, published by Chelsea Green, itself a 100% ESOP-owned company.

We began as a partnership in 1975, became a sole proprietorship in 1984, and restructured in 1987. On January 1, 1987, I signed SMC over to a new worker cooperative corporation. My compensation for selling the company was preferred shares based on a valuation (which were converted to cash over a period of five years) and a full ownership share. There were seven other employees at the time of the re-structuring; all were on a track to ownership. [There are 32 employees today.]

There are three principal criteria that prospective owners are expected to meet: an understanding and intent that employment at South Mountain will be their primary work for the foreseeable future; a demonstrated ability, from the annual evaluation process, to work effectively and cooperatively; and a commitment to understanding and honoring the company's core values: quality work, ethical business conduct, environmental responsibility, and concern for others—in short, we expect that a new owner will be a good representative of the company.

Ownership eligibility begins once an individual has worked a minimum of five years and 6,000 hours. During that time our personnel committee clarifies, before each individual reaches eligibility, whether the employee wishes to accept the responsibility and whether the current owners wish to accept this person as a partner. Employees are evaluated for ownership suitability and educated about the meaning of ownership.

Each owner has a full voice in the governance of the company. All policy decisions are made by consensus by the employee owners. There is a back-up 75% super-majority mechanism in case of consensus stalemates. This has occurred only three times in our 25 year history of cooperative ownership; each time it was resolved by a super-majority vote.

An important part of the SMC system is personal equity building through owners' annual profit sharing. Equity is accounted for in individual Internal Capital Accounts. These are paper accounts backed up by the company's net worth, not cash accounts.

Equity accounts begin with the membership fee that each owner pays; they grow at the end of each profitable year (every year so far!). The membership fee is for the purchase of a share of SMC ownership. Originally, we decided this needed to be significant but affordable. If it was too steep it would discourage participation, so we set it at the price of a good used car, an expense everyone seems to be able to manage when necessary. At the initial 1987 re-structuring it was set at $3,500. It escalates at a rate determined by the Owners; as of April 2014, it is $13,500. The fee may be paid in cash, or payments may be spread, at no interest, over a period of time not to exceed 36 months. When the fee is paid, it is used to open the new owner's individual capital account. At this point, this has become an uncommonly good investment for new owners. Equity distributions often equal or exceed the buy-in fee the first year.

Roughly fifty percent of net income is distributed as dividends among the owners, based on hours worked during that calendar year (this is distinct from the cash profit sharing that is extended to all employees each year in the form of wage bonuses). At least 20% of dividends must be in cash, and the entire dividend is taxable income to each individual, even the non-cash portion. The board makes certain that the cash portion is enough to at least cover the increased income tax liability generated from the cash distribution, so as to not cause a financial hardship to the individual owners.

The equity accounts continue to mature until the end of an individual's employment. The funds in these accounts are, except in special circumstances, inaccessible until an individual leaves the employ of the company. When an employee owner departs the company begins to pay out the equity amount with payments spread over eight years. A departing owner can elect a shorter payout period; if so, the distribution is at a discounted rate (immediate payout: 60%; two year payout: 72.5%; four year payout 79.5%; and six year payout 86.5%). Equity accounts are non-interest bearing.

In 1999 we established a special investment fund to use to pay off owners as they leave in the future. We build this account aggressively and invest the funds in socially responsible venues. We have made a commitment to always keep an amount of cash equal to at least 50% of total accumulated owners' equity and we maintain a 25 year spreadsheet to predict payments and assure that the fund will always be solvent. These reserves are the foundation of the stake that each of us has been earning and we consider our obligation to our fellow employee owners to be among our most essential responsibilities as a company.

Namasté Solar

Namasté Solar is a 62-employee solar installation company in Boulder, Colorado. Founded in 2005 by Blake Jones and two others, Namasté has always been a highly democratic, worker-owned company. From the outset, Jones set the company up as a one-person, one-vote basis on most issues other than key shareholder decisions, which were one-owner, one-vote. In Namasté's first couple of years, decisions were made by consensus, but as the company grew, decisions were made more by votes of employees, with a supermajority threshold of 60% for certain key issues, such as selling the company (employees turned down several lucrative offers in 2008, for instance).

Initially, Namasté was structured as a conventional stock corporation in which employees could buy shares at a fixed price of $5,000, which they can finance out of wages over time. Jones wanted the price to be higher, but employees outvoted him. On January 1, 2011, Namasté Solar became a formal worker-owned cooperative. Now all votes are one-owner, one-vote.

Namasté explains that "our intention is to share the entire experience of small business ownership; not just rewards (profits) and control, but also risks (losses) and responsibilities." Its Web site explains that "stock must be purchased and is never granted, gifted, or given as compensation. Only employees can own common stock. Each employee can only own one share of common stock (one person, one vote)." Employees become eligible after a 12-month trial period. They then must be voted in by their peers. The $5,000 share purchase does not appreciate or depreciate in value. When employees leave the company, their common stock must be redeemed at the original purchase price. The company may pay in cash or promissory note (typical term is one to four years).

The common stock ownership provides basic governance rights and the right to a share of the profits paid into a trust that employees can receive on departure. In addition, the company has preferred stock that can be bought by investors and/or employees. There are two classes of preferred stock. Preferred stock ownership is not tied to employment. There is no limit on how much employees and external investors may purchase. The preferred stock also does not appreciate or depreciate in value, but pays an annual target dividend rate of 6.5%, provided the company can make the payments out of earnings. Preferred stock has an annual target dividend of 6.5% and does not appreciate or depreciate.

The Namasté model tweaks the typical worker cooperative structure by introducing preferred stock to raise capital. Like most other worker cooperatives, however, its ownership focus is on shared governance and profits rather than stock price growth. A basic principle of these cooperatives is that focusing on stock price growth creates a potentially expensive repurchase obligation than can force the company to make decisions about its future it does not want to make. By limiting stock price growth, the company hopes to retain its democratic structure in the long term.

5

Profit Sharing and Stock Bonus Plans

Corey Rosen

WHILE ESOPS HAVE SUBSTANTIAL TAX BENEFITS, they also have more restrictive rules than other kinds of broad-based ownership plans. The next chapter in this book examines the use of profit sharing plans for employee ownership in detail. The present chapter provides a brief summary of the issues for both profit sharing and stock bonus plans, including a tabular side-by-side comparison.

As this chapter is being completed, there are about 7,000 statutory employee stock ownership plans (ESOPs) in the U.S., but also about 2,000 profit sharing plans and about 50 stock bonus plans that are at least 20% invested in company stock and have five or more plan participants, plus another 3,600 profit sharing plans and a handful of stock bonus plans with fewer than five employees.

Like ESOPs, profit sharing plans and stock bonus plans are governed by the Employee Retirement Income Security Act (ERISA). They are governed by plan trustees who have a fiduciary obligation to operate the plan in the best interests of plan participants. In all forms of defined contribution plans, company contributions to the plans are tax-deductible, and employee contributions are excluded from reportable income in the year they are contributed. All defined contribution plans must provide that employees receive a distribution after termination, death, disability, or retirement, although ESOPs and stock bonus plans have somewhat stricter rules than profit sharing plans.

There are some significant differences, however. ESOPs have substantial additional tax benefits beyond the deductibility of contributions, most notably the ability of sellers to certain ESOPs to defer capital gains taxes, the deductibility of dividends paid on ESOP shares, the ability to use dividends or (in S corporations) distributions of earnings to increase the allowable contribution limits, and, in S corporations, not paying income tax on that proportion of ownership attributable to the ESOP. Also, only ESOPs can borrow money from or on the credit of the company to buy employer stock.

Stock bonus plans operate very similarly to ESOPs in terms of their rules, with the major exception being that they do not have to be primarily invested in company stock. Instead, they only must offer employees the option to be paid out in the form of company stock. Because they are so similar in terms of rules but have fewer tax benefits, they are now rarely used as an alternative to ESOPs. Profit sharing plans have much less restrictive rules than ESOPs, however, including those for distributions, required diversification opportunities at age 55 and 10 years of service, valuation requirements, and what percentage of assets must be held in company stock.

A major difference between profit sharing and both ESOPs and stock bonus plans is that profit sharing plans allow much more flexibility in allocation rules. ESOPs and stock bonus plans generally must allocate benefits based on relative pay or a more level formula (one favoring lower-paid people). Under Treasury Regulation § 1.401(a)(4)-8(b)(1)(vi)(B), however, profit sharing (as well as 401(k) plans) can use age weighting (a formula that provide additional points for older employees) and/or comparability testing, where testing is done on projections of future benefits. Profit sharing plans can also be integrated with Social Security, meaning they can offset part of the benefits based on what

Social Security pays. All of that means that profit sharing plans can be used to provide more benefits to higher-paid people than ESOPs and stock bonus plans.

In general, companies not needing to borrow money through the plan, not using the plan to provide the seller the special tax deferral treatment available to sellers to C corporation ESOPs, wanting to favor more highly paid people, and/or not wanting to be an S corporation to obtain the special S corporation ESOP tax benefits may find there are no special benefits to having a statutory ESOP.

Table 5-1 on the following pages summarizes the key differences between these plans.

Companies Using Profit Sharing Plans

Hy-Vee

Hy-Vee is one of the largest supermarket chains in the U.S., with 234 stores and 56,000 employees throughout the Midwest. It was started in Iowa in 1930. From the outset, the company shared profits with employees and only allowed employees to own shares. The company's leaders wanted the company to stay a very private company, however. The company was able to avoid the necessity for registering its securities by staying under 500 shareholders and complying with applicable exemptions for limited offerings of stock. Laws at the time did not require extensive financial disclosure to employees, but by the 1960s, anti-fraud disclosure requirements became stricter, meaning the company would have to divulge a great deal of information to employees. Concerned that such information might leak out to competitors or other parties it did not want to have this information, the company decided to limit the number of people who could own shares.

It still wanted broad employee ownership, however. The solution was to set up a qualified profit sharing trust. The company would contribute profits to the plan to buy company stock for plan participants. The company decided to limit ownership in the plan to 15% of the total

Table 5-1. Plan types compared

Plan type	ESOPs	Profit sharing plans	Stock bonus plans
Key tax benefits			
Deductibility of employer contributions to the plan	Deductible up to 25% of eligible compensation. In C corporations, contributions made to pay interest on an ESOP loan generally do not count toward this limit.	Deductible up to 25% of eligible compensation (profit sharing plans cannot borrow money from the company or use its credit to buy company stock, so the interest exclusion does not apply).	Deductible up to 25% of eligible compensation (profit sharing plans cannot borrow money from the company or use its credit to buy company stock, so the interest exclusion does not apply).
Deductibility of dividends	Dividends are deductible if used to repay an ESOP loan, are passed through to participants, or are voluntarily reinvested in company stock by employees.	Dividends paid on shares are not deductible.	Dividends paid on shares are not deductible.
Tax benefits to owners	Sellers can defer taxation of gains from a sale to an ESOP in a C corporation that owns at least 30% of company stock after the sale.	No tax benefits to sellers to the plan trust.	No tax benefits to sellers to the plan trust.
Taxation of ownership by plan in S corporation	Allocation of corporate income to the ESOP based on ESOP ownership is not subject to current taxation on the ESOP.	Plan trusts must pay unrelated business income tax on their attributed corporate income based on ownership.	Plan trusts must pay unrelated business income tax on their attributed corporate income based on ownership.
Employee taxation	Taxed in the same way as other defined contribution plans based on distributions from the plan not otherwise rolled over to another qualified plan or an IRA.	Taxed in the same way as other defined contribution plans based on distributions from the plan not otherwise rolled over to another qualified plan or an IRA.	Taxed in the same way as other defined contribution plans based on distributions from the plan not otherwise rolled over to another qualified plan or an IRA.

Table 5-1. Plan types compared

Plan type	ESOPs	Profit sharing plans	Stock bonus plans
Rules			
Borrowing money	Can borrow money from the company or use its credit to buy employer stock.	Cannot borrow money from the company or use its credit to buy employer stock.	Cannot borrow money from the company or use its credit to buy employer stock.
Governance	Trust is governed by a plan trustee who must operate the plan for the exclusive benefit of plan participants.	Trust is governed by a plan trustee who must operate the plan for the exclusive benefit of plan participants.	Trust is governed by a plan trustee who must operate the plan for the exclusive benefit of plan participants.
Voting	Plan participants must be able to direct the trustee as to the voting of the shares on a limited number of issues, most significantly the sale of all or substantially all the assets of the employer.	No voting requirements.	Same voting requirements as for ESOPs if more than 10% of plan assets are in company stock; otherwise no voting requirements.
Distribution timing	Generally, must offer distribution commencing within six years after end of plan year for termination unless termination is for death, disability or retirement, in which case distribution must begin not later than one year after the end of the plan year after termination.	Must begin by normal retirement age but it is rare for plans to wait that long.	Generally, must offer distribution commencing within six years after end of plan year for termination unless termination is for death, disability, or retirement, in which case distribution must begin not later than one year after the end of the plan year after termination.

Table 5-1. Plan types compared

Plan type	ESOPs	Profit sharing plans	Stock bonus plans
Rules (continued)			
Form of distribution	Employee must have the right to demand distributions in the form of company stock unless company is an S corporation or has bylaws requiring that all or substantially all the shares be held by employees.	Can be in stock or cash.	Employee must have the right to demand distributions in the form of company stock unless company is an S corporation or has bylaws requiring that all or substantially all the shares be held by employees.
Eligibility and vesting	Rules are generally same as for other defined contribution plans.	Rules are generally same as for other defined contribution plans.	Rules are generally same as for other defined contribution plans.
Allocation	Generally must allocate based on relative compensation or a more level formula; integration with Social Security, age weighting, and comparability testing not allowed.	In addition to normal allocation rules that apply to ESOPs and stock bonus plans, companies can integrate benefits with Social Security, age-weight allocations, or use comparability testing based on projected future benefits.	Generally must allocate based on relative compensation or a more level formula; integration with Social Security, age weighting, and comparability testing not allowed.
Put option	Employees must have a put option on shares distributed to them.	Not applicable.	Employees must have a put option on shares distributed to them.

Table 5-1. Plan types compared

Plan type	ESOPs	Profit sharing plans	Stock bonus plans
Rules (continued)			
Required investment in company stock	Plan must be primarily invested in company stock with the highest combination of voting and dividend rights.	No minimum requirement; plan can hold any class of shares.	No minimum requirement; plan can hold any class of shares.
Valuation	Required annually by statute.	Not required by statute, but strongly advised for fiduciary protection.	Not required by statute, but strongly advised for fiduciary protection.
Fiduciary concerns	Subject to close scrutiny by DOL with respect to valuation and prohibited transaction rules.	Subject to close scrutiny by DOL with respect to valuation and prohibited transaction rules; also subject to scrutiny relative to prudence and diversification.	Subject to close scrutiny by DOL with respect to valuation and prohibited transaction rules.

shares of the company, partly out of concern that employee accounts be sufficiently diversified. Eventually, the company changed the plan to a 401(k) plan (these did not exist until the 1970s and did not become common until the 1980s). The company now makes a match of 50% up to the first 6% of employee deferrals into the plan. Part of that match is in company stock, with the company maintaining its limit of 15% of total company stock in the plan.

For Hy-Vee, an ESOP would not offer any additional tax benefits not available with the existing plan structure. The company does not pay dividends (deductible in an ESOP), and the ESOP does not own enough of the company (30%) to qualify employees to sell to the plan and take a tax deferral on the gain. There is also no need to borrow money through the plan.

Southwest Airlines

Southwest Airlines is the only major airline to record consistent profits over the last few decades. It is the only major airline that has not declared bankruptcy or laid off people. Unlike all the other major airlines, it has also never had a strike. Flying Southwest is a distinctly different experience from flying other airlines. Employees are given considerable leeway to make their own decisions about how to serve—and amuse—customers. Employees work in teams with more decision-making autonomy than at other carriers. Southwest consistently ranks at or near the top in customer satisfaction and is frequently cited as a best place to work.

Southwest has periodically provided all employees with stock options, but its core ownership sharing tool is a profit sharing plan. The plan allows Southwest more flexibility in the mix of assets in the plan than an ESOP would. According to its 2012 Form 5500 filing with the Department of Labor, there was $357 million in employer stock out of $2.1 billion in total assets in the plan.

The profit sharing plan provides a percentage of profits will contributed annually to the plan. It typically is about 7% to 8% of pay. Some of that goes into employer stock and the rest into other assets. Employees own about 10% of the total shares. In addition to the profit sharing plan, employees can buy stock through an employee stock purchase plan with a 10% discount.

Hollister

As noted above, one of the key reasons companies choose profit sharing plans instead of ESOPs is that the regulations are less strict. One of the most important aspects of this is that, unlike ESOPs, profit sharing plans are not required to have an outside appraiser determine the value of shares. Many advisors, as well as the NCEO, strongly advise that any closely held company with stock in a defined contribution plan should do this in any event to lessen fiduciary risk and make sure that transactions are done at a reasonable price, but there is no statutory requirement for an appraisal. Hollister, Inc., is a 2,400-employee closely held company in Illinois that develops, manufactures, and markets medical devices in the fields of ostomy, continence care, and wound care. It is an interesting example of a company that had significant employee ownership in its profit sharing plan and used book value rather than an appraised value to determine share price. Employees eventually challenged that practice in court, but the court sided with Hollister. Material in this section was drawn from the court documents and Hollister's Web site; the company prefers not to provide any additional details.

Hollister's plan controls about 95% of the shares. It has been an exceptionally good investment, with stock price increasing at 28% per year between 1997 and 2010 and 13% between 2010 and 2012. Employees average over $350,000 in allocations. The plan is entirely funded by the company. Hollister's bylaws limit ownership to the profit sharing plan and to current and former employees. The plan uses "profit sharing accounting" for the shares, meaning each employee has an allocated interest in the total value of the plan's assets rather than a specific number of shares and other assets.[1] As a result, employees do not receive a distribution of shares from the plan. Instead, their distribution is a dollar amount reflecting their account balance. Shares are sold back to Hollister in the plan each year based on projected cash needs to handle the distributions.

The plan specified that the price for the shares was the book value as of the most recent month. The bylaws specify that the employees can transfer shares subject to a company right of first refusal on the shares. There is no indication in the materials when employees are able to ask for a transfer, although the issue has become moot, as explained below. The initial payment is limited to $250,000, with the remainder as a promissory note. The participants have routinely had distributions that have far exceeded this $250,000 amount. Because ERISA prohibits

---

1. ESOPs can use the same approach if the plan provides for it. The purpose of this approach is that it effectively automatically rebalances everyone's percentage of stock versus cash holdings at the end of the year so that all participants have the same percentage of stock and cash, other than shares they have chosen to diversify once they have met the diversification requirements (profit sharing plans have no such diversification requirements).

a non-ESOP plan from accepting a promissory note, the employees have not been able to use the transfer mechanism.

Instead, the company has relied on an "exceptional circumstances" clause that allows it to make an annual determination of how much the plan will need to fund redemptions of shares. It will then contribute enough money at the beginning of the year to do that based on the most recent year-end book value.

A group of employees eventually sued over the valuation issue. In *DeFazio v. Hollister, Inc.*, 854 F. Supp. 2d 770 (E.D. Cal. 2012), a district court sided with the company. The plaintiffs argued that either the shares should have been redeemed at the most recent monthly book value as specified in the plan under the transfer option, or the company should have had an outside appraisal done to determine the purchase value. The monthly book value had been increasing each month for the period in question. The plaintiffs hired a well-known ESOP appraiser as an expert witness; the appraiser argued that the proper approach to appraisal should have been based on a willing financial buyer/willing seller model, as in an ESOP, a model that would rely heavily on projections of future earnings.

The court sided with the defendants. It acknowledged that "although § 1108(e) and case law interpreting it have never required trustees to obtain an independent audit, the Ninth Circuit has recognized that 'securing an independent assessment from a financial advisor or legal counsel is evidence of a thorough investigation.'" Despite that, the court concluded that there was no persuasive evidence that the use of year-end book value would produce a significantly different result from an appraisal. Although it agreed with plaintiffs that the fiduciaries failed to conduct a thorough investigation of the issue, it nonetheless refused to award damages to the plaintiffs.

The case should be read to provide only limited comfort on the valuation issue for profit sharing plan trustees. The court clearly indicated that a more thorough and independent investigation would be a more prudent standard. Most courts opining on valuation issues have looked primarily to procedures, not results, even if the results, as in this case, provide very favorable for participants.

6

Profit Sharing Plans as an Alternative to ESOPs

Cynthia A. Moore and Christopher T. Horner II

ESOPS AND PROFIT SHARING PLANS are employee benefit plans that are governed by the Employee Retirement Income Security Act of 1974, as amended (ERISA), and the Internal Revenue Code of 1986, as amended (the "Code") and fall within the concurrent jurisdiction of the U.S. Department of Labor and the Internal Revenue Service (IRS). ESOPs and profit sharing plans are defined contribution retirement plans.[1] Both types of plans must satisfy certain legal

1. A defined contribution plan is a plan in which an employer commits to making contributions to participant accounts. In the case of a defined contribution plan there is no guaranteed retirement benefit; the retirement benefit is based exclusively upon the contributions to the plan and the earnings attributable to such contributions. In contrast, in a defined benefit plan participants (and spouses) are guaranteed a certain level of retirement benefit typically determined by reference to an individual participant's wages and duration of service with the employer.

requirements to receive preferential federal tax treatment.[2] Unlike profit sharing plans, ESOPs are designed to invest primarily in employer securities. Profit sharing plans can be invested in employer securities in one or more of the following ways: (1) an employer securities fund can be offered as an investment alternative in a plan where a participant directs the investment of his or her account balance; (2) a plan sponsor can make part or all of its contribution to the profit sharing plan in the form of employer securities; and (3) a plan sponsor that makes all investment decisions for a profit sharing plan can choose to hold employer securities as one of the plan's investments.

Employer contributions to a profit sharing plan need not be made from current or accumulated profits.[3] A profit sharing plan must provide a definite, predetermined formula for allocating the contributions made to the plan among the participants and for distributing the funds after a fixed number of years, the attainment of a stated age, or upon the occurrence of some event such as layoff, illness, disability, retirement, death or separation from service.[4]

Although profit sharing plans and ESOPs are subject to many of the same rules, ESOPs generally have more favorable tax treatment but are also subject to more restrictive rules than profit sharing plans, as described below.

Deductible Contributions

ESOPs and profit sharing plans are defined contribution plans that entitle the employer sponsoring the plan to a deduction in the amount of the contribution in the taxable year in which the contribution is made.[5] The law imposes the same limitation on the amount that may be

2. For example, ESOPs and profit sharing plans are subject to the same rules governing eligibility and vesting.
3. Code § 401(a)(27)(A).
4. Treas. Reg. § 1.401-1(b)(1)(ii).
5. See, e.g., Code § 404(a)(3)(A) (S corporation ESOPs and profit sharing plans); Code § 404(a)(9) (C corporation ESOPs).

properly deducted by the employer; employer contributions to either an ESOP or a profit sharing plan are deductible up to 25% of covered payroll.[6] One significant difference arises in the case of a C corporation sponsoring a leveraged ESOP, in which case the 25% limitation does not include employer contributions made to enable the ESOP to amortize interest under an exempt loan.[7] Moreover, the law permits a C corporation to make a deductible contribution up to an additional 25% of covered compensation to the ESOP, provided this amount is not used to amortize principal or interest under the exempt loan.[8] The deduction limitations for an S corporation are the same as the limitations for a C corporation, except that the 25% limitation includes employer contributions made to enable the ESOP to amortize interest under an exempt loan.[9]

Deductible Dividends

Congress also bestowed ESOPs with a number of significant tax advantages relating to the payment of dividends that profit sharing plans do not enjoy. For example, a C corporation is entitled to a deduction for dividends declared and paid on employer securities owned by an ESOP, provided a number of legal requirements are satisfied.[10] To be

6. Id.

7. Code § 404(a)(9)(B).

8. See, e.g., PLR 9548036 (Sept. 7, 1995) (the IRS ruled that the limitations under Code Section 404(a)(3) and Code Section 404(a)(9)(A) are applied separately).

9. See Code §§ 404(a)(3) and (a)(9). Section 404(a)(9) of the Code permits an employer to make contributions in excess of 25% of covered payroll provided that such contributions are used to amortize interest under an exempt loan. However, Section 404(a)(9) of the Code applies only to C corporations sponsoring ESOPs. See Code § 404(a)(9)(C) ("This paragraph shall not apply to S corporations"). As a result, S corporations are subject to the deduction limitation imposed under Section 404(a)(3) of the Code, which does not permit an employer to make contribution in excess of 25% of covered payroll, even if such contributions are used to amortize interest under an exempt loan.

10. Code § 404(k). An S corporation sponsoring an ESOP is not entitled to a deduction for distributions declared and paid on employer securities owned by the ESOP. Id.

deductible, the dividend must be paid directly to participants and beneficiaries, paid to the ESOP and passed through to participants and beneficiaries, reinvested in employer securities at the direction of participants and beneficiaries, or used to satisfy the ESOP's obligations under an exempt loan.[11]

The deduction on account of dividends is not subject to the 25% limitation discussed above. Furthermore, a dividend must be "reasonable" in order to be properly deductible.[12] In contrast, distributions declared and paid by an S corporation on shares owned by the ESOP are not deductible.[13] The deductibility of dividends is a significant tax benefit afforded to a C corporation that maintains an ESOP. ESOP companies frequently declare and pay dividends on employer securities owned by the ESOP to fund the company's repurchase obligation or repay an exempt loan made to the ESOP.[14]

Unlike a C corporation sponsoring an ESOP, an employer declaring and paying a dividend on employer securities held by a profit sharing plan is not entitled to a deduction.[15]

---

11. Code § 404(k). Note that for a dividend to be deductible on account of being used to amortize an exempt loan, it must be declared and paid on shares purchased with the proceeds of the exempt loan being amortized. Id.

12. See Code § 404(k)(5)(A) (disallowing the dividend deduction if the dividend constitutes, in substance, an evasion of taxation). The legislative history of Code Section 404(k) suggests that the reasonableness of a particular dividend is evaluated in terms of a reasonable compensation test. See H.R. Rep. Conf. No. 841, 99th Cong., 2d Sess. (1986). The IRS has ruled that the standard is what the corporation can be expected to pay on a recurring basis, and a reasonable dividend does not include an unusually large dividend used to amortize an exempt loan. See TAM 9304003 (Sept. 30, 1990).

13. Code § 404(k) (explicitly limiting the dividend deduction to C corporations).

14. Id.

15. To be deductible, the dividend must be declared and paid on "applicable employer securities" which are held by an employee stock ownership plan (as opposed to any other qualified plan). See Code § 404(k)(3).

Section 1042: Deferral of Recognition of Long-Term Capital Gain

One of the most significant differences between an ESOP and a profit sharing plan is the ability of an ESOP to afford a taxpayer the opportunity to defer recognition of the long-term capital gain realized by such taxpayer in connection with the sale of his or her stock to the ESOP.[16] The ability to do this is subject to various requirements, the analysis of which is beyond the scope of this chapter. These requirements include: (1) the plan sponsor must be a C corporation at the time of the sale, (2) the ESOP must own at least 30% of the outstanding stock of the plan sponsor immediately following the sale, and (3) the taxpayer must reinvest his or her sale proceeds in qualified replacement property within the qualified replacement period.[17] A profit sharing plan does not provide a taxpayer with an analogous tax deferral.[18]

Unrelated Business Income Tax

Profit sharing plans are subject to federal taxation on unrelated business taxable income (UBTI), whereas ESOPs are not. The effect is to reduce the benefits distributable to participants and beneficiaries of a profit sharing plan in an amount equal to the unrelated business income tax (UBIT) liability of the tax-exempt trust forming a part of the profit sharing plan. This distinction is relevant in the context of an S corporation sponsoring an ESOP. As discussed below, the portion of taxable income of the S corporation allocated to the ESOP is exempt from UBIT, whereas the same portion of taxable income of

16. See generally Code § 61 (defining gross income); see also Code § 1042 (nonrecognition provision applying to qualified employer securities sold to an ESOP).

17. See, e.g., Code § 1042.

18. The nonrecognition provision of Section 1042 of the Code applies only to sales of qualified employer securities to ESOPs and certain eligible worker-owned cooperatives. See Code § 1042(b)(1).

the S corporation allocated to the profit sharing plan is considered UBTI subject to UBIT.

Before 1950, a tax-exempt entity, such as an employee benefit trust, could operate a business unrelated to its tax-exempt purposes without incurring a federal tax liability, based on the premise that all income used to support charitable purposes was tax-exempt.[19] Congress imposed a tax on UBTI of tax-exempt trusts to address concerns regarding unfair competition.[20] Generally, UBTI of the tax-exempt trust forming a part of a profit sharing plan is subject to UBIT.[21] UBTI includes gross income derived from a trade or business the conduct of which is not substantially related to the purpose of the tax-exempt trust.[22]

The enactment of the Small Business Jobs Protection Act of 1996 enabled ESOPs to be permitted S corporation shareholders.[23] In addition, the legislation imposed UBIT on the S corporation income allocated to the tax-exempt trust forming a part of an ESOP. The practical effect was to impose two levels of taxation for S corporation income allocated to the tax-exempt trust (one level on the UBTI of the tax-exempt trust itself and one level on distributions to participants and beneficiaries), compared to one level of taxation for income allocated to individual S corporation shareholders. Congress responded by passing the Taxpayer Relief Act of 1997, which exempted ESOPs from UBIT.[24] Congress did not exempt profit sharing plans holding employer securities in an S corporation from UBIT. For this reason, it is generally impractical for a profit sharing plan to hold employer securities of its S corporation sponsor.

19. H.R. Rep. 2319, 81st Cong. 2d Sess. 36 (1950), 950-2 C.B. 412.

20. Code § 511; Treas. Reg. §1.513-1(b).

21. Code § 511.

22. Code § 513(a).

23. Pub. L. 104–188, H.R. 3448, 110 Stat. 175.

24. Code § 512(e)(3); Pub. L. 105–34, H.R. 2014, 111 Stat. 787.

Federal Taxation of Benefit Distributions and Net Unrealized Appreciation

The federal tax consequences of benefits distributed to participants of a profit sharing plan and an ESOP are the same. As a general rule, benefit distributions to a participant or beneficiary of a qualified plan are taxable to the participant or beneficiary in the taxable year in which benefits are distributed.[25] One exception to this rule is if the participant rolls the distribution over to an individual retirement account (IRA) or another qualified plan that accepts rollover distributions. In this case, the participant is not currently taxable. The rollover benefits are taxed at ordinary income rates when the benefits are distributed from the IRA or qualified plan.

Participants in both profit sharing plans and ESOPs are subject to an early withdrawal penalty tax.[26] If the participant is under age 59½ (or age 55 if the participant has terminated employment), the participant is subject to an excise tax equal to 10% of the benefit distributed.[27]

The law affords favorable tax treatment of lump-sum distributions of employer securities from a qualified plan, including both profit sharing plans and ESOPs. Section 402(e) of the Code excludes from gross income the net unrealized appreciation of the employer securities during the time it was held by the qualified plan.[28] In other words, the Code allows a participant to take a lump-sum distribution of employer securities from a qualified plan, pay ordinary income tax on the cost basis (in the hands of the qualified plan), and pay long-term capital gain taxes on the amount constituting the net unrealized appreciation.[29]

---

25. Code § 402(e).
26. Code § 72(t).
27. See Code § 72(t)(2) for exception to the general rule.
28. Code § 402(e)(4)(B).
29. To be clear, the participant would not be taxed on the net unrealized appreciation until the participant disposes of the employer securities.

Prohibited Transactions and Exemptions

ERISA prohibits certain transactions between a plan and parties in interest regardless of whether the transaction is fair or beneficial to the plan. Congress perceived such transactions as inherently risky and subject to abuse.[30] Both ESOPs and profit sharing plans are subject to the prohibited transaction rules under ERISA and the Code. However, ESOPs are unique in that they can borrow money from, or on the credit of, the employer to buy employer securities. And along with profit sharing plans, ESOPs can invest up to 100% of plan assets in qualifying employer securities and can acquire qualified employer securities from a party in interest.

Extension of Credit or Guaranty of Extension of Credit

Generally, ERISA and the Code prohibit a fiduciary of an employee benefit plan from causing the plan to engage in a transaction that constitutes the lending of money or extension of credit between the plan and a party in interest (including the employer).[31] ERISA imposes personal liability on the *fiduciary* who breaches its duty, and requires that such fiduciary make good to the plan, any loss incurred by reason of its breach.[32] In contrast, the Code imposes an excise tax on any *dis-*

30. See, e.g., *Donovan v. Cunningham*, 716 F.2d 1455 (5th Cir. 1983) (purpose of prohibited transaction rules "was to make illegal per se the types of transactions that experience had shown to entail a high potential for abuse"); *M & R Investment Co. v. Fitzsimmons*, 685 F.2d 283 (9th Cir. 1982) (prohibited transaction rules are "a broad per se prohibition against transactions ERISA implicitly defines as not arm's-length"); *Cutaiar v. Marshall*, 590 F.2d 523 (3d Cir. 1979) ("Congress intended to create an easily applied per se prohibition of the type of transaction in question").

31. ERISA § 406(a)(1)(B); DOL Reg. § 2550.408b-3(a)(2) (prohibited transaction includes loan to ESOP that is guaranteed by a party in interest); see also Code § 4975(c)(1)(B); Treas. Reg. § 54.4975–7(b)(1)(ii) (prohibited transaction includes loan to ESOP that is guaranteed by a disqualified person).

32. ERISA § 409(a). Additionally, the fiduciary must restore to such plan any profits made by it through the improper use of plan assets. Id. Finally, a fiduciary is

qualified person who engages in a prohibited transaction.[33] An initial excise tax of 15% of the amount involved in a prohibited transaction for each year in the taxable period is imposed on the disqualified person.[34] In the case of an impermissible lending of money or extension of credit between a plan and a disqualified person, the amount involved equals the greater of the interest paid or the fair market value of the interest under the credit facility.[35]

Congress exempted ESOPs from this general rule to the extent that the lending of money or loan qualifies as an "exempt loan."[36] As a result, an ESOP can finance the acquisition of employer securities with the proceeds of an exempt loan made to it; this is known as a "leveraged ESOP."[37] Congress did not exempt profit sharing plans from the application of this rule.

---

subject to other equitable and remedial relief, including injunctions and removal, attorney's fees, and interest. Id.

33. The Code does not impose liability on a fiduciary that is acting only in a fiduciary capacity. In addition, unlike the prohibited transaction rules under ERISA, the Code does not require the disqualified person to have had knowledge of the prohibited transaction.

34. Code § 4975(a). In the event the prohibited transaction is not corrected within the taxable period, the Code imposes a tax equal to 100% of the amount involved on the disqualified person who participated in the prohibited transaction. See Code § 4975(b). The "taxable period" begins on the date of the prohibited transaction and ends on the earliest of (1) the date a notice of deficiency under Code § 6212 is mailed; (2) the date on which the 15% tax under Code § 4975(a) is assessed; or (3) the date on which the prohibited transaction is corrected. Code § 4975(f)(2).

35. Treas. Reg. § 53.4941(e)-1(b)(2)(ii).

36. ERISA § 408(b)(3); DOL Reg. § 2550.408b-3; Code § 4975(d)(3); Treas. Reg. § 54.4975–7(b); Treas. Reg. § 54.4975-11. Among other requirements, an exempt loan must be made primarily for the benefit of the participants and beneficiaries of the ESOP; must be at a reasonable rate of interest; and any collateral securing the ESOP's obligations under an exempt loan consists only of certain qualifying employer securities. Code § 4975(d)(3); Treas. Reg. § 54.4975-7(b).

37. Code § 4975(d)(3).

Diversification of Plan Assets

With limited exceptions, ERISA requires a fiduciary of an employee benefit plan to diversify plan assets.[38] Generally, an employee benefit plan is prohibited from acquiring or holding employer securities with a fair market value in excess of 10% of plan assets.[39] An exception from this general rule exists for an eligible individual account plan (EIAP).[40] Both ESOPs and profit sharing plans are included within the definition of an EIAP, provided that the plan explicitly provides for the acquisition and holding of qualifying employer securities.[41] In fact, Congress designed ESOPs "to invest primarily in employer securities."[42] The term "primarily" is undefined. The U.S. Department of Labor has stated that there may be instances where a fiduciary would breach its fiduciary duties if it invested more than 50% of plan assets in qualifying employer securities.[43] The Department of Labor concluded that the "primarily" requirement must be satisfied over the life of the ESOP.[44] As a result, both an ESOP and a profit sharing plan can be designed to invest 100% of their assets in qualifying employer securities.

Sale or Exchange of Property

In addition to prohibitions on the lending of money or extension of credit, ERISA and the Code prohibit a fiduciary from engaging in a transaction that constitutes the sale or exchange of property with a party in interest.[45] As with the lending of money or extension of credit, ERISA imposes personal liability on the *fiduciary* who breaches its

---

38. ERISA § 404(a)(1)(C).
39. ERISA § 407(a).
40. ERISA § 407(d)(3)(B).
41. Id.
42. Code § 4975(e)(7).
43. DOL Advisory Opinion 83–6A (January 24, 1983).
44. Id.
45. ERISA § 406(a)(1)(A).

duty, and requires that such fiduciary make good to the plan, any loss incurred by reason of its breach.[46] In contrast, the Code imposes an excise tax on any *disqualified person* who engages in a prohibited transaction.[47] An initial excise tax of 15% of the amount involved in a prohibited transaction for each year in the taxable period is imposed on the disqualified person.[48] In the case of an impermissible sale or exchange of property between a plan and a disqualified person, the amount involved equals (1) the greater of the amount of money and the fair market value of the other property given by the plan and (2) the amount of money and the fair market value of the other property received by the plan.[49]

Congress exempted plans (both ESOPs and profit sharing plans) from this general prohibition to the extent that the sale or exchange satisfies certain legal requirements.[50] First, the plan must be acquiring or selling qualifying employer securities.[51] Second, the acquisition or sale must be for adequate consideration.[52] Third, no commission can

46. ERISA § 409(a). Additionally, the fiduciary must restore to such plan any profits made by it through the improper use of plan assets. Id. Finally, a fiduciary is subject to other equitable and remedial relief, including injunctions and removal, attorney's fees, and interest. Id.

47. The Code does not impose liability on a fiduciary that is acting only in a fiduciary capacity. In addition, unlike the prohibited transaction rules under ERISA, the Code does not require the disqualified person to have had knowledge of the prohibited transaction.

48. Code § 4975(a). In the event the prohibited transaction is not corrected within the taxable period, the Code imposes a tax equal to 100% of the amount involved on the disqualified person who participated in the prohibited transaction. See Code § 4975(b).

49. Code § 4975(f)(4).

50. ERISA § 408(e); DOL Reg. 2550.408e; Code § 4975(d)(13).

51. ERISA § 408(e). The term "qualifying employer securities" is defined in ERISA § 407(d)(5).

52. ERISA § 408(e)(1). The term "adequate consideration" is defined in ERISA § 3(18) and DOL Prop. Reg. § 2510.3-18(b).

be charged in connection with the acquisition or sale.[53] Finally, the plan must constitute an eligible individual account plan.[54]

Administration

Eligibility

The same eligibility requirements apply to all qualified retirement plans, including ESOPs and profit sharing plans.[55] Generally, the Code and ERISA permit a qualified plan to require that an employee complete one year of service and attain age 21 before becoming eligible to participate.[56] A qualified plan may permit earlier participation if the employer so desires.

Vesting

The same vesting requirements apply to all qualified retirement plans, including ESOPs and profit sharing plans.[57]

Allocations

Contributions (whether in the form of employer securities or cash) to an ESOP are allocated to eligible plan participants as the ESOP receives the contributions. In contrast, employer securities acquired by an ESOP with exempt loan proceeds are placed in a suspense account to be allocated to participant accounts as the loan is amortized.[58] As the exempt loan is repaid, employer securities are released from a

53. ERISA § 408(e)(2).
54. ERISA § 408(e)(3). The definition of an eligible individual account plan includes an ESOP and a profit sharing plan. See note 41 and accompanying text.
55. See Code § 410(a).
56. Code § 410(a)(1)(A); ERISA § 202(a)(1)(A).
57. Code § 401(a)(7); Code § 411(a); ERISA § 203(a)(2)(B).
58. Treas. Reg. § 54-4975-7(b).

suspense account based on the "applicable release fraction," which is a fraction based on either (1) principal and interest payments or (2) principal payments only.[59] The *release* of employer securities from the suspense account must be distinguished from the *allocation* of employer securities to participants' employer securities accounts.

Generally, allocations of contributions (whether in the form of employer securities or cash) must be based on a participant's compensation relative to the compensation of all participants in the ESOP. In addition, allocations of employer securities might be based on a more level formula. Integration with Social Security taxable wages and cross-testing, discussed below, are not permissible allocation methodologies for ESOPs.[60]

In a profit sharing plan, a participant must first satisfy any conditions to receive an allocation for a plan year, typically completing 1,000 hours of service and employment on the last day of the plan year. The employer's profit sharing contribution can be discretionary or fixed and is allocated to participants in the manner set out in the plan document. Allocation methods include:

1. pro rata on the basis of each participant's compensation relative to the total compensation of all participants entitled to receive an allocation for the plan year (up to the annual limit on compensation under Section 401(a)(17) of the Code);
2. the contribution can be "integrated" under Section 401(l)(2) of the Code, such that a participant with wages above the Social Security taxable wage base receives a larger contribution;
3. each participant can be given "points" for age, service, and/or compensation, with allocations being made in proportion to each

---

59. Treas. Reg. § 54.4975–7(b)(8)(i)-(ii). An applicable release fraction based on principal payments only results in low allocations of employer securities in the early years of the loan, when primarily interest is being paid off.

60. Code § 401(a)(4); Treas. Reg. § 1.401(a)(4)-2(b).

participant's total points relative to all participants' total points; and

4. the allocation can be based on a "cross-tested" formula, in which different classes of participants are established and the contribution is made on a percentage basis to each class.[61]

Code Section 415 Limits

The Code limits the amount of "annual additions" that can be allocated to all of the defined contribution plan accounts of each participant in a limitation year.[62] Annual additions include employer contributions, employee elective deferrals, and certain forfeitures.[63] A participant cannot receive annual additions in excess of the lesser of a dollar limit ($52,000 as of 2014) and 100% of eligible compensation, up to $260,000 (as of 2014; these limits are adjusted for cost-of-living increases).[64]

A special rule applies to leveraged ESOPs sponsored by C corporations. Under this special rule, if no more than one-third of the employer contributions are allocated to highly compensated employees, the employer contributions that are used to amortize interest under the exempt loan and allocated forfeitures of employer securities that were acquired with the proceeds of the exempt loan are excluded from the calculation of annual additions.[65]

In addition, in the case of a leveraged ESOP, annual additions can be calculated based on employer contributions used by the ESOP to amortize an exempt loan or based on the fair market value of the

---

61. A cross-tested profit sharing plan satisfies the nondiscrimination test of Code § 401(a)(4) by demonstrating that the benefits (rather than the contributions) do not discriminate in favor of highly compensated employees. Treas. Reg. § 1.401(a)(4)-8(b). An ESOP is not permitted to demonstrate nondiscrimination with respect to benefits. Treas. Reg. § 1.401(a)(4)-8(b)(1)(i).
62. Code § 415(a)(1)(B).
63. Code § 415(c)(2).
64. Code § 415(c)(1)(A); Code § 401(a)(17).
65. Code § 415(c)(6).

employer securities allocated to participants' employer securities accounts.[66]

Annual additions calculated with respect to employer contributions do not consider appreciation in the employer securities' value from the time such securities are placed into the suspense account.[67] In addition, dividends or distributions declared and paid on employer securities held by an ESOP constitute earnings and generally do not constitute annual additions.[68] Nonetheless, the Internal Revenue Service is empowered to recharacterize amounts that an employer designates as dividends or distributions if it determines that such dividends or distributions are appropriately treated as annual additions.[69]

Profit sharing plans are ineligible for this special rule and thus are subject to the normal annual addition limits.

Valuation

The Code requires that all defined contribution plans, including ESOPs and profit sharing plans, must provide for a valuation of investments held by the trust, at least once a year, on a specified date, in accordance with a method consistently followed and uniformly applied.[70] Moreover, the Code provides that an ESOP is not a qualified plan unless all valuations of employer securities that are not readily tradeable on an established securities market, with respect to activities carried on by the ESOP, are performed by an independent appraiser.[71] A valuation

66. Treas. Reg. § 1.415-6(g)(4) and Notice 87-21, Q&A 11.
67. Treas. Regs. §§ 1.415-6(g)(4), 54.4975–11(a)(8)(ii) and 54.4975–7(b)(8)(iii).
68. PLR 200243055 (Feb. 20, 2003); see also Treas. Reg. § 1.415-2(b)(1)(iv).
69. See, e.g., *Steel Balls, Inc. v. Commissioner*, 69 TCM 2912, *aff'd* 89 F.3d 841 (8th Cir. 1996) (unpublished per curiam).
70. Rev. Rul. 80-155, 1980-1 C.B. 84; Treas. Reg. § 1.415-6(g)(4); Notice 87-21, Q&A 11.
71. Code § 401(a)(28)(C).

by an independent appraiser is not required in the case of employer securities that are readily tradeable on an established securities market.[72]

Although profit sharing plans are not required to obtain an annual valuation by an independent appraiser, a profit sharing plan must value non-publicly traded employer securities on an annual basis to comply with its obligations under both ERISA and the Code. Form 5500 must reflect the "current value" of all plan assets, including employer securities, as of the first and last day of the plan year and must also reflect unrealized appreciation and depreciation of plan assets.[73] "Current value" means the fair market value where available. Otherwise, it means the fair value as determined in good faith by a trustee or a named fiduciary, assuming an orderly liquidation at the time of the determination.[74] Furthermore, an accurate assessment of fair market value is essential for a plan's ability to comply with certain requirements in the Code, such as the exclusive benefit rule of Section 401(a)(2), the annual limit on contributions under Code Section 415, and the deduction rules under Code Section 404.[75] Finally, the valuation of a profit sharing plan's assets will determine the value of a participant's account and, ultimately, the amount of his or her distribution.

Distributions

Timing of Payment

Both profit sharing plans and ESOPs are subject to the general rules governing distributions from qualified benefit plans. However, ESOPs are subject to a second set of rules for stock the plan acquired after 1986 (which nowadays often means all the stock that an ESOP holds).

72. See Treas. Reg. § 54.4975-7(b)(1)(iv) (defining the term "readily tradeable on an established securities market").
73. ERISA § 103(b)(3)(A); Instructions to Schedule H of Form 5500.
74. ERISA § 3(26).
75. Internal Revenue Manual Section 4.72.8.1.

In any given situation, the set of rules that would mandate an earlier distribution apply; usually it is the special ESOP rules that do so.

Under the general rules applying to both profit sharing plans and ESOPs, unless otherwise elected by the participant, distributions must begin no later than 60 days after the end of the plan year in which the latest of the following events occurs: (1) the date on which the participant attains the earlier of age 65 or the normal retirement age specified under the plan; (2) the 10th anniversary of the year in which the participant commenced participation in the plan; or (3) the date the participant terminates from service with the employer.[76] If the participant's account balance is greater than $5,000, the participant's consent is generally required before a distribution can be made.[77] If a participant elects a distribution, it is generally payable within the time period specified in the plan document, which may be as soon as administratively feasible after the distribution is elected. However, if the plan holds non-publicly traded employer securities, distributions may be restricted until after the annual valuation of employer securities has been performed, so that the account value is properly determined.

Under the special ESOP rules, distributions usually begin sooner than they would under the general rules above. A participant can elect, with the consent of his or her spouse, to commence distribution of benefits from an ESOP not later than one year after the close of the plan year in which the participant separates from service by reason of the attainment of normal retirement age under the plan, disability, or death, or the close of the plan year that is the fifth plan year following the plan year in which the participant separates from service for any other reason.[78] The rules governing the commencement of distributions represent the legal limit on how long the employer can postpone distributing benefits from an ESOP to a participant. Applicable law permits an employer to adopt more liberal rules governing the tim-

---

76. Code § 401(a)(14).
77. Code § 411(a)(11).
78. Code § 409(o)(1)(A). These rules assume the participant is not reemployed by the employer before commencement of distributions.

ing of distributions. In addition, the "financed securities exception" provides that the distribution of employer securities acquired with the proceeds of an exempt loan may be delayed until the close of the plan year in which such exempt loan is repaid in full.[79]

Both ESOPs and profit sharing plans may provide for in-service distributions after a fixed number of years (after contributions have been held in the plan for at least two years)[80] or upon a bona fide hardship.[81] However, ESOPs generally do not permit in-service distributions.

Both ESOPs and profit sharing plans must permit a direct rollover to an IRA or other qualified plan in accordance with Section 401(a)(31) of the Code. Further, both ESOPs and profit sharing plans are subject to the required minimum distribution rules of Section 401(a)(9) of the Code which provides that distributions must begin by the April 1 after the later of the year in which the participant attains age 70½ or retires.[82]

Method of Payment

Unless an ESOP participant elects otherwise, distributions must be distributed in substantially equal periodic payments (at least annually) over a period not to exceed five years.[83] However, if the participant's account balance exceeds $1,050,000 (as of 2014), the distribution period is increased, unless the participant elects otherwise, to five years plus one additional year (up to five additional years) for each $210,000 (as of 2014), or fraction thereof, by which the balance exceeds $210,000

79. Code § 409(o)(1)(B). Discussion regarding the applicability of the financed securities exception is beyond the scope of this chapter.

80. Rev. Rul. 71-295, 1971-2 C.B. 184.

81. Rev. Rul. 71-224, 1971-1 C.B. 124.

82. Notwithstanding the general rule, required minimum distributions to a 5% owner must begin no later than the April 1 after the calendar year in which the individual attains age 70½. Code § 401(a)(9)(C)(ii).

83. Code § 409(o)(1)(C)(i).

(as of 2014; this and the other dollar figures are adjusted for cost-of-living increases).[84]

Profit sharing plans are exempt from the qualified joint and survivor annuity (QJSA) rules if (1) the plan provides that the participant's vested benefit is payable in full, upon the participant's death, to the participant's surviving spouse, unless the participant elects, with the spouse's consent, that such benefit be paid instead to a designated beneficiary; (2) the participant does not elect the payment of benefits in the form of a life annuity; and (3) the plan is not a transferee or an offset plan.[85]

Unless a profit sharing plan is subject to the QJSA rules, the Code does not specify any particular form of distribution from the plan, and distributions are made in the form specified in the plan document. Distributions are typically permitted in the form of a lump sum, periodic installments (not to exceed the life expectancy of the participant or the joint life expectancies of the participant and his/her beneficiary), or in an annuity form, as elected by the participant.

Form of Payment

Distributions from an ESOP may be made in the form of cash, subject to the participants' right to demand distribution in the form of employer securities.[86] Two exceptions to this general rule exist. First, if the employer's corporate charter or bylaws restrict the ownership of substantially all outstanding employer securities to employees or to a trust under a qualified plan, the participant may be precluded from demanding a distribution in the form of employer securities.[87] Second, participants in an ESOP sponsored by an S corporation may be also be precluded from demanding a distribution in the form of employer

84. Code § 409(o)(1)(C)(ii).

85. Treas. Reg. § 1.401(a)-20, Q&A 3.

86. Code § 409(h)(1)(A).

87. Code § 409(h)(2)(B)(ii)(I).

securities.[88] Distributions in the form of employer securities that are not readily tradeable on an established securities market are subject to the put option rules discussed below.

Distributions from a profit sharing plan may be made in cash or in kind, as specified in the plan document. If the plan holds employer securities that are publicly traded, it is typically distributed in the form of stock.

Put Option

Employer securities distributed from an ESOP that are not readily tradeable on an established securities market or subject to a trading limitation must be subject to a put option.[89] The put option must permit a participant to "put" the employer security to the employer.[90] An ESOP cannot be obligated to honor a participant's put option, but the ESOP can have a right of first refusal to assume the employer's obligations of the put option.[91] With respect to timing, the put option must be exercisable for at least 60 calendar days following the date of the distribution and for at least an additional 60 calendar day period in the following plan year.[92]

If the participant receives a "total distribution" that is required to be repurchased by the employer, the employer must make payments in substantially equal periodic payments (at least annually) over a period beginning not later than 30 calendar days after exercise of the put option and not exceeding five years.[93] The employer must provide adequate security and pay reasonable interest on the unpaid amounts.[94]

---

88. Code § 409(h)(2)(B)(ii)(II).

89. See Code § 409(h); Treas. Reg. § 54.4975–7(b)(10).

90. Code § 409(h)(1).

91. Treas. Reg. § 54.4975-7(b)(9).

92. Code § 409(h)(4).

93. Code § 409(h)(5). A "total distribution" is a distribution within one taxable year to the recipient of the balance to the credit of the recipient's account. Id.

94. Id.

If the participant receives installment distributions that are required to be repurchased by the employer, the employer must remit payment for the employer securities no later than 30 calendar days after the put option is exercised by the participant.[95]

Employer securities distributed from a profit sharing plan are not required to be subject to a put option.

Diversification

ESOPs that acquired employer securities of private companies on or after January 1, 1987, are subject to certain diversification requirements.[96] Under these rules, a qualified participant is entitled to elect to diversify a portion of his or her ESOP account during the qualified election period. A qualified participant is an employee who has completed at least 10 years of participation under the ESOP and has attained age 55. The initial opportunity to elect must be offered within 90 calendar days after the close of the plan year in which the participant becomes a qualified participant. The amount must be distributed within 180 calendar days after the close of the plan year in which the election is made. The qualified election period is the 6-plan-year period commencing after a participant becomes a qualified participant. A qualified participant is eligible to diversify 25% of his or her employer securities account balance for the first 5 years of his or her qualified election period and 50% of his or her employer securities account during their sixth and final plan year. The diversification calculation is a cumulative calculation. In other words, the employer

---

95. Code § 409(h)(6). An exception to the general put option rule exists for ESOPs established and maintained by a bank or other financial institution that is prohibited by applicable law from redeeming its own securities. In this case, the employer securities are not required to be subject to a put option, provided that the participants have a right to receive distributions in the form of cash. See Code § 409(h)(3).

96. Code § 401(a)(28)(C). Certain ESOPs that hold publicly traded employer securities are subject to a different set of diversification rules. See Code § 401(a)(35) and the discussion below.

securities account balance consists of the number of eligible shares that have ever been allocated to a qualified participant's account less any shares previously distributed, transferred, or diversified. An employer can satisfy its diversification obligation by a distribution, a transfer to another qualified plan, or offering three or more investment options within the ESOP.[97]

Effective for plan years beginning on and after January 1, 2007, a profit sharing plan that holds publicly traded employer securities is subject to a different set of diversification rules.[98] Any "applicable individual" may elect to reinvest the portion of the account attributable to nonelective employer contributions and invested in employer securities in other investment funds. An individual is an "applicable individual" if he or she is a participant who has completed three years of service; is an alternate payee of a participant who has completed three years of service; or is the beneficiary of a deceased participant.[99] The plan must make available at least three investment options, other than employer securities, to which an applicable individual may direct the proceeds from the divestment of employer securities, each of which is diversified and has materially different risk and return characteristics.[100] Divestment and reinvestment may be limited to periodic, reasonable periods occurring at least on a quarterly basis.[101] Thus, unlike an ESOP, an applicable individual in a profit sharing plan holding publicly traded employer securities may choose to divest up to 100% of the portion of his or her account attributable to employer contributions out of employer securities on an ongoing basis. Employer securities held in a profit sharing plan sponsored by a private corporation are not subject to diversification rules.

Under Section 101(m) of ERISA, a plan administrator of a profit sharing plan holding publicly traded employer securities must provide

97. Code § 401(a)(28)(B)(ii).

98. Code § 401(a)(35).

99. Code § 401(a)(35)(C); Treas. Reg. § 1.401(a)(35)-1(c)(2).

100. Code § 401(a)(35)(D).

101. Code § 401(a)(35)(D)(ii)(I).

a notice to applicable individuals not later than 30 days before the first date on which the individuals are eligible to exercise their rights. The notice must set forth the diversification rights and describe the importance of diversifying the investment of retirement plan accounts.[102]

An ESOP that holds publicly traded employer securities is not subject to the diversification rules of Section 401(a)(35) of the Code if it is a separate plan from any other defined benefit or defined contribution plan maintained by the same employer and holds no contributions that are (or were ever) subject to Section 401(k) or 401(m) of the Code.[103] In other words, an ESOP is subject to these rules only if the ESOP is a portion of a larger plan (whether or not that plan holds contributions subject to Section 401(k) or 401(m)).[104]

Voting of Employer Securities

If the employer has a registration-type class of securities, the ESOP must pass through voting rights with respect to all qualifying employer securities that are entitled to vote and are allocated to participants' employer securities accounts.[105] Generally, the term "registration-type class of securities" means securities that are required to be registered under Section 12 of the Securities Exchange Act of 1934.[106]

If the employer has no registration-type class of securities, then the pass-through of voting rights is required only if the employer's stock is not publicly traded and more than 10% of the ESOP's assets consist of securities of the employer.[107] Pass-through of voting rights is required only if applicable state law requires one of the corporate matters enumerated in Section 409(e) of the Code to be submitted to

102. The Internal Revenue Service has provided a model notice that may be used for this purpose in Notice 2006-107.

103. Code § 401(a)(35)(E)(ii).

104. Treas. Reg. § 1.401(a)(35)-1(f)(2)(ii).

105. Code § 4975(e)(7); Code § 409(e)(2).

106. Code § 409(e)(4).

107. Code § 401(a)(22).

a shareholder vote.[108] A participant or beneficiary is entitled to vote all employer securities allocated to his or her employer securities account regardless of whether the participant is vested in such employer securities.

Participants are not entitled to vote unallocated employer securities; unallocated employer securities may be voted by participants and beneficiaries or a fiduciary.[109] The employer must furnish participants and beneficiaries and the ESOP fiduciaries with the same notices and information statements that the employer's charter, bylaws, or applicable federal or state law would require the employer to distribute to other shareholders.[110] Participants and beneficiaries are entitled to vote fractional rights to securities.[111] The fiduciary may vote the employer securities allocated to a participant's employer securities account for which no voting directive is received.[112]

An employer that does not have a registration-type class of securities may satisfy the requirements under Section 409(e)(3) of the Code if the plan provides for "mirror voting," whereby each participant is entitled to one vote with respect to each issue on which the participant has the right to vote, regardless of the number of employer securities allocated to such participant's employer securities account, and the fiduciary votes the employer securities held by the plan in proportion to the directive received from participants and beneficiaries.[113]

---

108. PLR 9705004 (Dec. 15, 1996); *Central Trust Co., N.A. v. American Avents Corp.*, 771 F. Supp. 871, 876 (S.D. Ohio 1989); *Schoenholtz v. Doniger*, 657 F. Supp. 899, 905 (S.D.N.Y. 1987). Such events may include a merger, recapitalization, liquidation, dissolution, or sale of substantially all assets.

109. Treas. Reg. § 1.46-8(d)(8)(i).

110. Treas. Reg. § 1.46-8(d)(8)(ii).

111. Treas. Reg. § 1.46-8(d)(8)(iii).

112. See DOL Op. Ltr. Re: Carter Hawley Hale Stores, Inc. (Apr. 30, 1984); see also Rev. Rul. 95-57, 1995-2 C.B. 62 (concluding that voting by fiduciary of allocated employer securities for which no direction was received is not inconsistent with Section 409(e)(2) and (3) of the Code).

113. Code § 409(e)(5).

A profit sharing plan is not required to pass through voting rights on employer securities held in the plan to participants and beneficiaries.[114] However, a participant-directed individual account plan that is intended to comply with Section 404(c) of ERISA will often pass through voting rights to ensure that the participant is exercising "control" over his or her account.[115] If voting rights are not passed through to participants, the trustee of the plan will vote the shares, either in its discretion or, in the case of a directed trustee, by following the direction of the employer or plan administrator.

Conclusion

Profit sharing plans are a viable alternative to ESOPs as vehicles of facilitating employee ownership. Much like an ESOP, a well-drafted profit sharing plan may invest any portion of its assets in employer securities and may distribute benefits to participants and their beneficiaries in the form of employer securities. As a result, a simpler, more flexible profit sharing plan might accomplish the same goals that a complex ESOP can accomplish. An ESOP should be used where specific objectives exist that only an ESOP can achieve, such as providing an owner with a liquidity event and allowing him or her to defer gain on the sale of stock under Section 1042 of the Code.

114. Code § 401(a)(22) (explicitly carving profit sharing plans out of the defined contribution plans required to satisfy the voting provisions of Section 409(e) of the Code).

115. DOL Reg. §2550.404c-1(c)(1)(ii).

About the Authors

Christopher T. Horner II is a founding member of Holzman Horner PLLC and has dedicated his career to counseling shareholders, boards of directors, and executives of closely held businesses in connection with liquidity strategies, business succession planning, and corporate governance matters. In addition, Chris represents ERISA fiduciaries and lenders in connection with a variety of matters relating to ESOPs. Chris is also a managing director of AmbroseAdvisors, a middle-market investment bank and financial advisory firm advising business owners with business succession planning, liquidity strategies, and capital placements. Before cofounding Holzman Horner PLLC, Chris was a member of the mergers and acquisitions and federal taxation practice groups in the Washington, D.C., office of an AmLaw 200 law firm. Chris received his juris doctor from the University of Virginia School of Law. He received his BA degrees magna cum laude in both economics & commerce and Greek & Latin from Hampden-Sydney College.

Cynthia A. Moore is a member resident in Dickinson Wright's Troy, Michigan, office and director of the firm's Regulatory–Administration division. She is a national expert on fringe benefit plans and is counsel to many plan sponsors in the design and administration of qualified retirement plans and welfare benefit plans. She also counsels companies and compensation committees on the tax, ERISA, and securities law aspects of executive compensation programs, such as supplemental executive retirement plans, stock option plans, restricted stock plans, and non-qualified deferred compensation plans. Ms. Moore received her BA from Alma College and her JD from The University of Texas at Austin.

Corey Rosen is the NCEO's founder and former executive director and now is its senior staff member. Corey has spoken on various subjects related to employee ownership all over the world with government, business, and union leaders, and he is regularly quoted in leading magazines and newspapers. He has appeared on national television and radio programs and also has authored five books on employee ownership, plus more than 100 articles for various business, academic, and professional publications. He has authored or coauthored many of the NCEO's practical and research publications. He holds a PhD in political science from Cornell University.

About the NCEO

The National Center for Employee Ownership (NCEO) is a nonprofit organization that has supported the employee ownership community since 1981. Our mission is to help employee ownership thrive. We have more than 3,000 members because we help people make smart decisions about employee ownership, with everything from reliable information on technical issues to helping companies reach the full potential of employee ownership.

Members receive the members-only newsletter *Employee Ownership Report* as well as access to weekly webinars and a library of prerecorded webinars; members-only website resources, including the Document Library, ESOP Q&A, and more; discounts on books and other NCEO products and services; and the right to contact the NCEO for answers to questions. See www.nceo.org/join for details or to sign up. See www.nceo.org/publications to browse and buy our books.

Made in the USA
Monee, IL
04 November 2026

67378111R00046